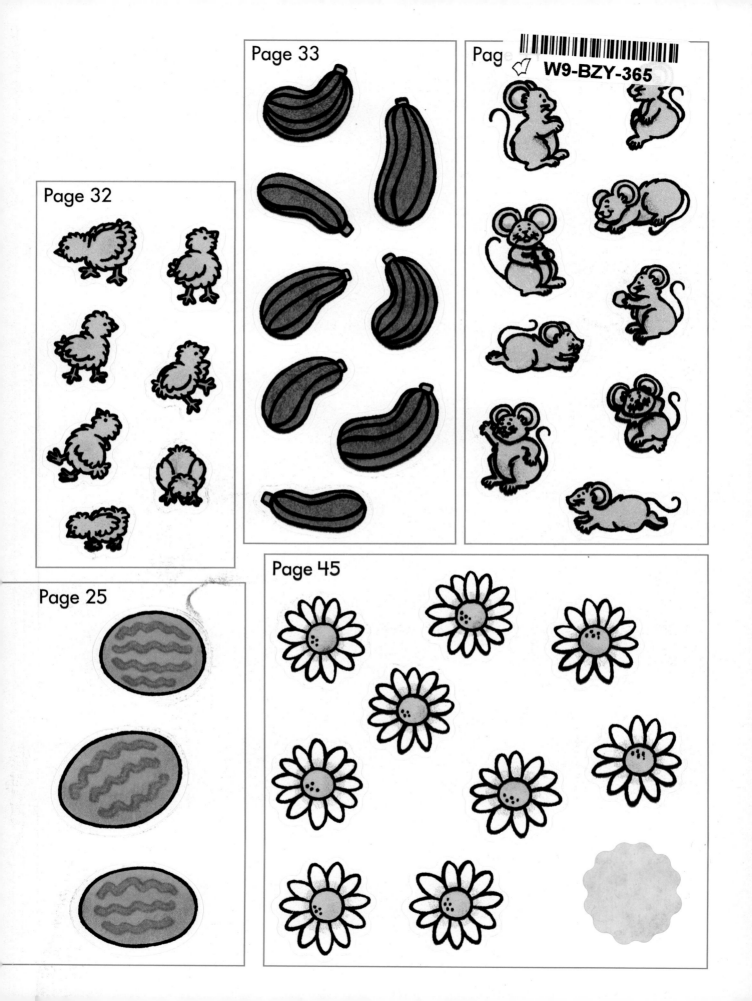

Page 33

Page 32

W9-BZY-365

Page 45

Page 25

You're number 1!

 Draw a picture of yourself.

Count 1 . Color 1 .

horse   horse

|

Color I and one.

Count 2  . Color 2 .

COWS   **COWS**

2

 Color **2** and **two**.

Find 1  sticker. Add it to the picture.
Color the picture.

6

Find 2 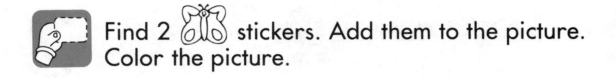 stickers. Add them to the picture. Color the picture.

Count 3 🐐. Color 3 🐐.

goats   goats

3

8

Skill: recognizing the numeral 3 and the number word <u>three</u>

Count 4  kittens. Color 4 kittens.

4

Color **4** and **four**.

Find 3  stickers. Add them to the picture.
Color the picture.

Find 4 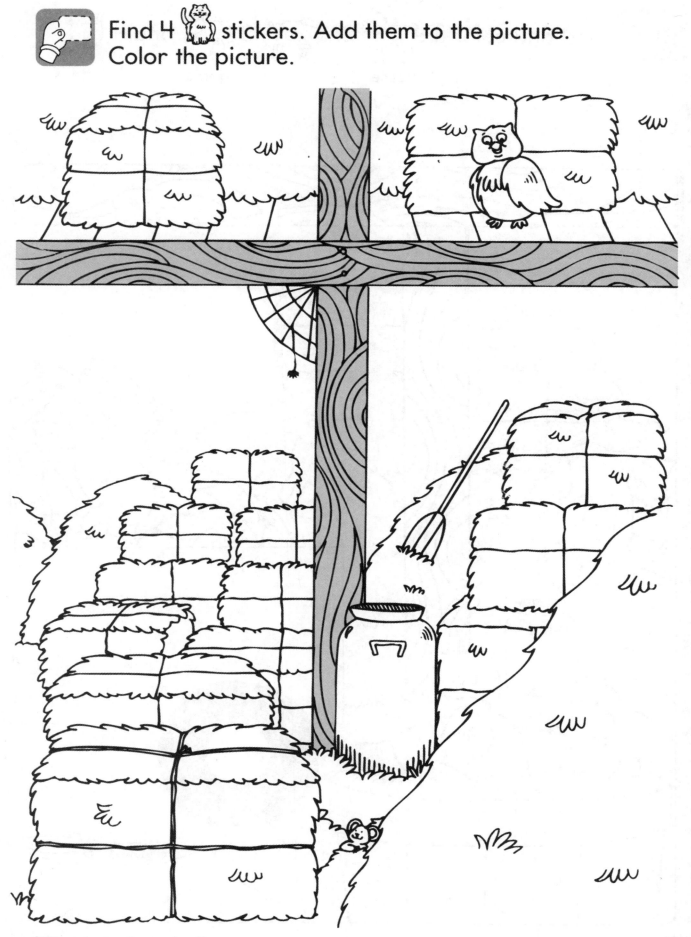 stickers. Add them to the picture.
Color the picture.

Find and color 1 , 2 ⬤, 3 ⬤, and 4 ⬤.

horse   cows   goats   kittens

Count 5 🐑. Color 5 🐑.
sheep   sheep

5

Skill: understanding the number 5

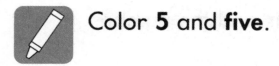 Color **5** and **five**.

5

five

Count and match the animals and the number. Draw a line.

Count and match. Draw a line.

1

2

3

4

5

Count and match. Draw a line.

1

2

3

4

5

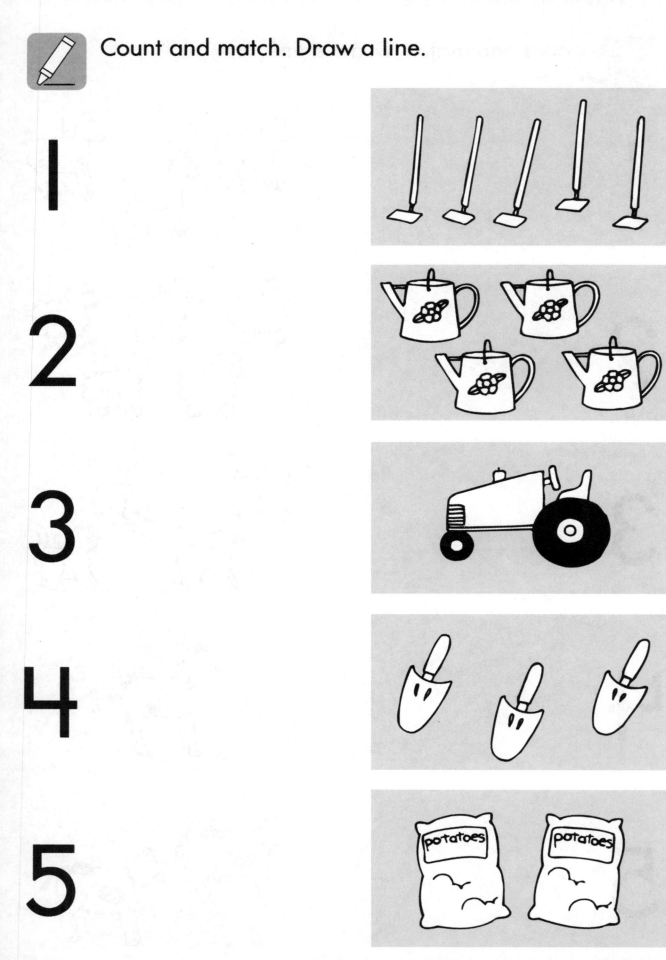

Skill: using 1 to 1 correspondence to review the numbers 1 to 5

Match the numbers. Draw a line.

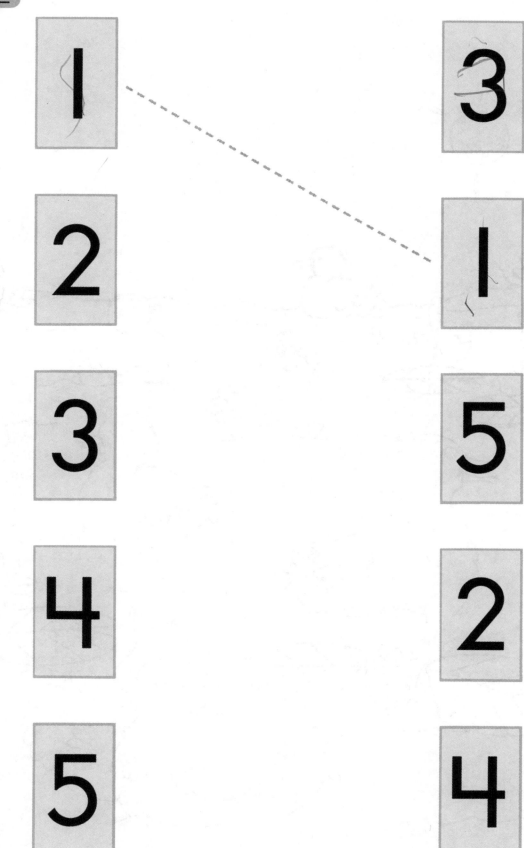

Count 6 . Color 6 .

ducks   ducks

6

Color **6** and **six**.

Find 5  stickers. Add them to the picture.
Color the picture.

Find 6  stickers. Add them to the picture.
Color the picture.

Watermelons

Find and color 5 🐑 and 6 🦆.

sheep   ducks

Count 7  . Color 7  .
dogs   dogs

7

Skill: understanding the number 7

Color **7** and **seven**.

Count 8 pigs. Color 8 pigs.

8

<u>Skill:</u> understanding the number 8

Color **8** and **eight**.

Find 7  stickers. Add them to the picture.
Color the picture.

Find 8  stickers. Add them to the picture. Color the picture.

Count and match. Draw a line.

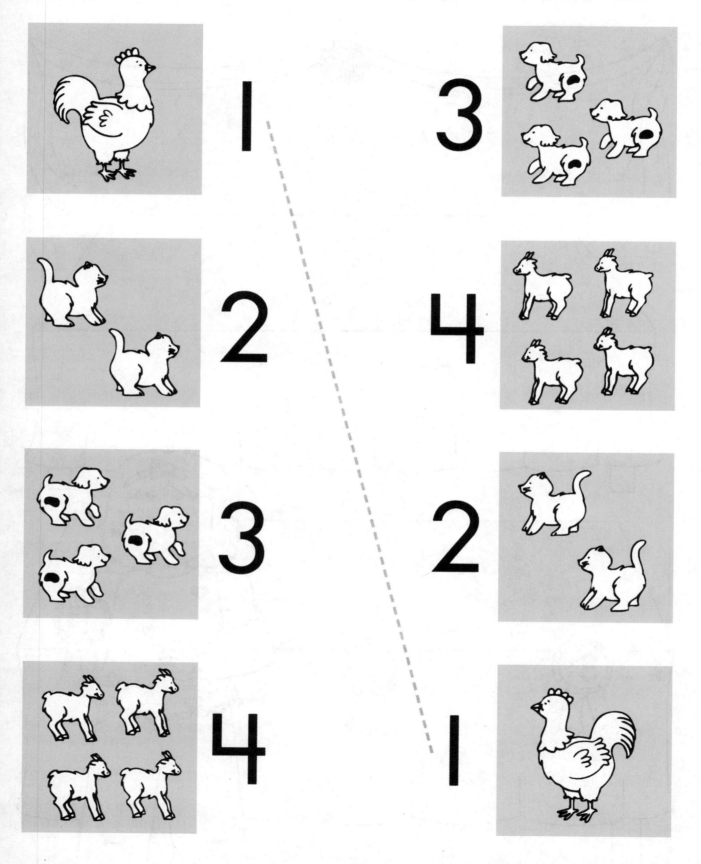

Count and match. Draw a line.

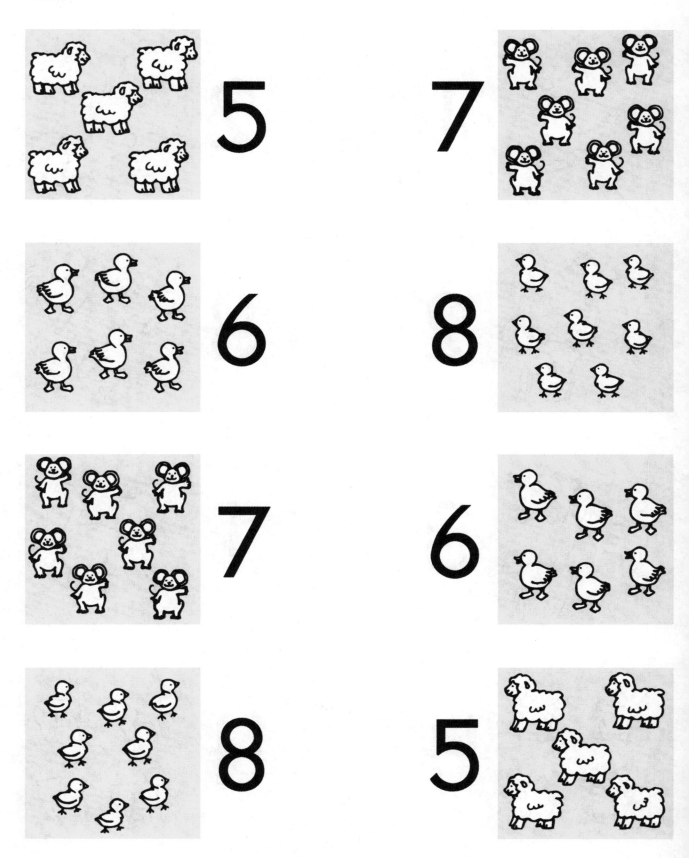

5

7

6

8

7

6

8

5

Count and match. Draw a line.

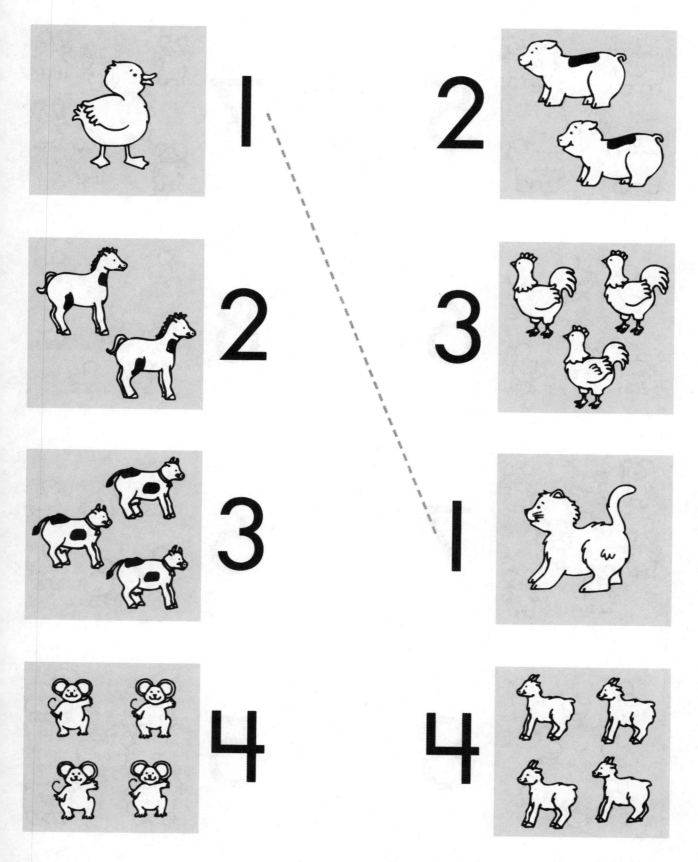

Count and match. Draw a line.

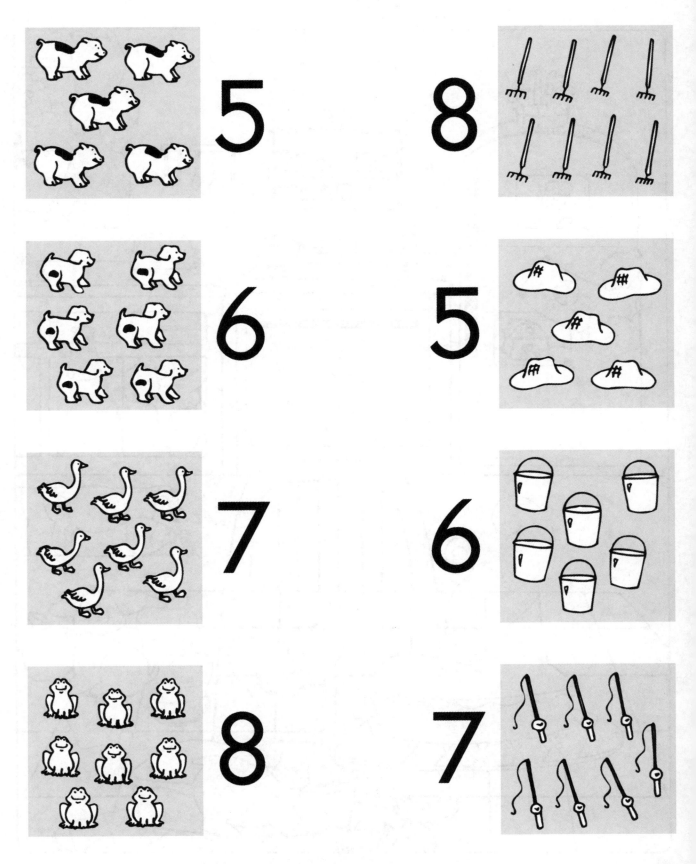

Find and color 7 puppies.

Skill: reviewing the number 7

Find and color 8 .

pigs

Count 9 . Color 9 .
chicks   chicks

q

Skill: understanding the number 9

Color **9** and **nine**.

Count 10 . Color 10 . rabbits rabbits

10

Color **10** and **ten**.

Find 9  stickers. Add them to the picture.
Color the picture.

welcome

44

Find 10 🌼 stickers. Add them to the picture.
Color the picture.

Count and match. Draw a line.

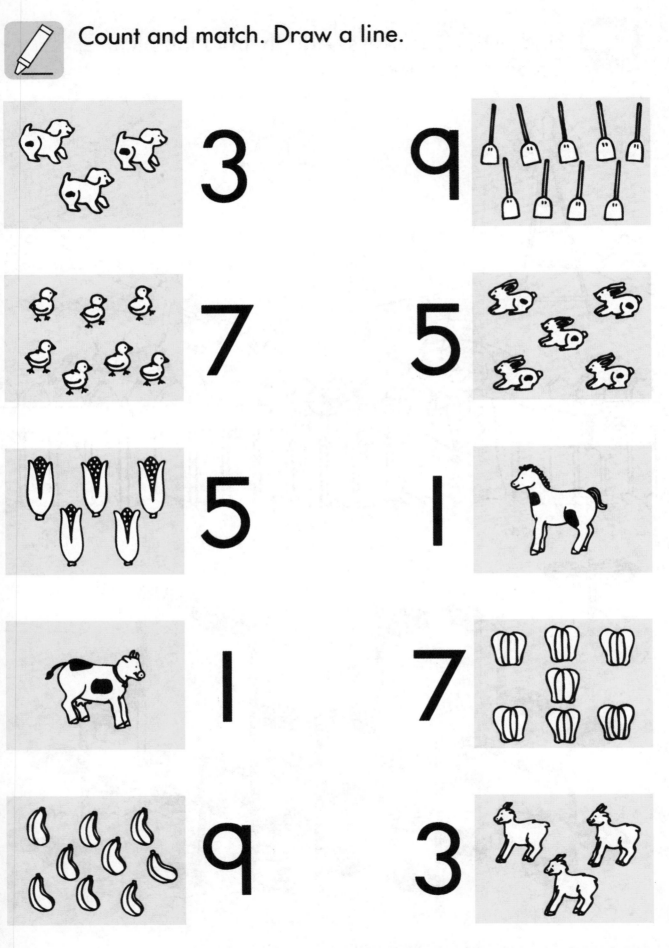

Skill: using 1 to 1 correspondence to review the numbers 1 to 10

Count and match. Draw a line.

2

8

10

6

4

2

8

4

6

10

Find and color 9 chicks.

Noodles

jelly jelly jelly
jam jam jam

yams

pears   pears

peas

beans

potatoes
10 lbs.

48

Skill: reviewing the number 9

Find and color 10 .

rabbits

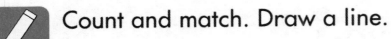

Count and match. Draw a line.

1

2

3

4

5

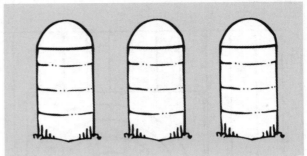

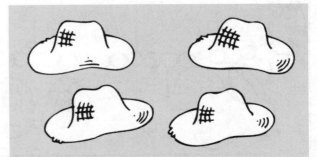

Skill: using 1 to 1 correspondence to review the numbers 1 to 5

Count and match. Draw a line.

6

7

8

q

10

Follow the numbers from 1 to 10 to find a home for the animals.

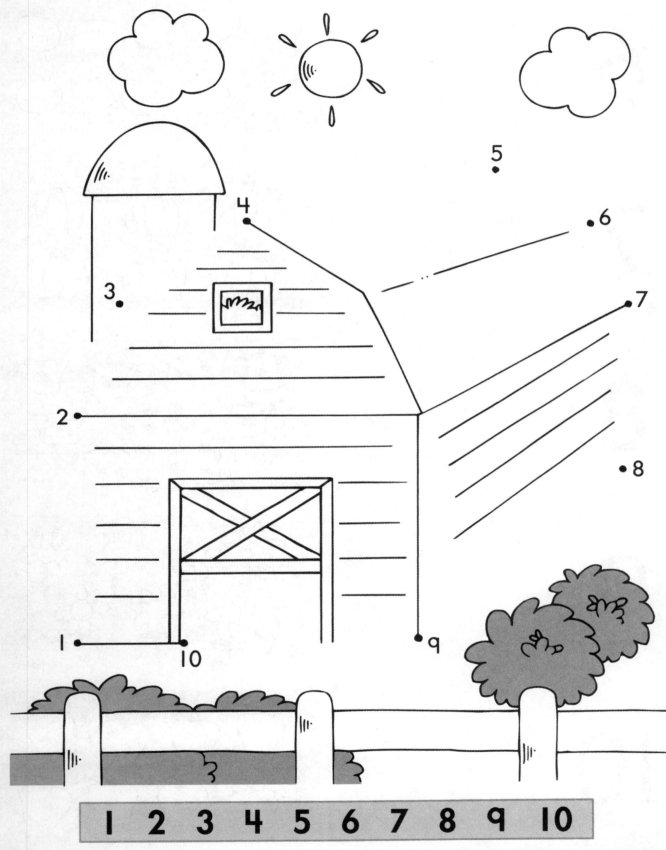

| 1 | 2 | 3 | 4 | 5 | 6 | 7 | 8 | 9 | 10 |

Draw the correct number of eggs in each nest.

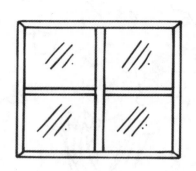

8   5   2

7   4   3

Draw the correct number of apples in each basket.

Draw 10  on the vine.
pumpkins

Pumpkins

Follow the numbers from 1 to 10 to get the cow to the barn.

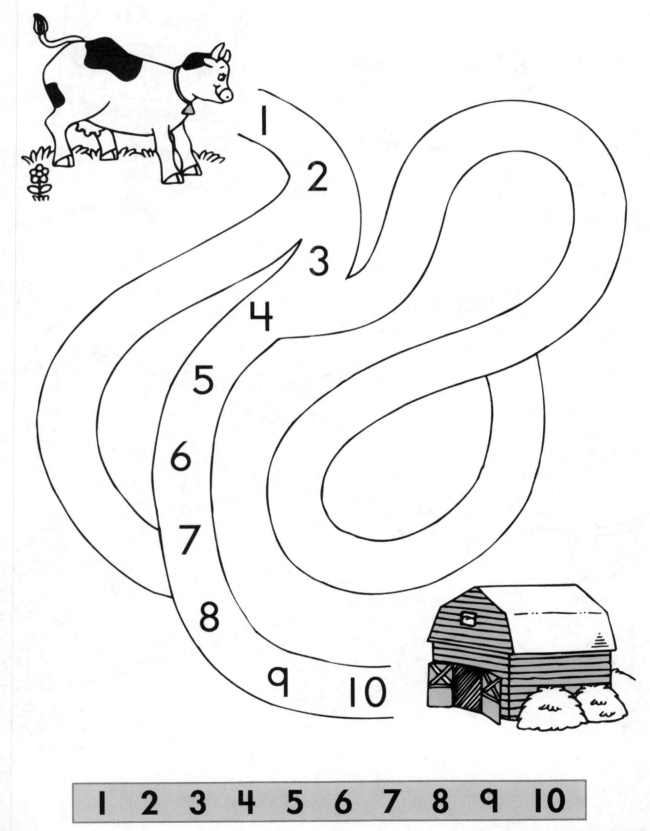

| 1 | 2 | 3 | 4 | 5 | 6 | 7 | 8 | 9 | 10 |

Skill: reviewing the numbers 1 to 10

Follow the numbers from 1 to 10 to get the hen to her chicks.

| 1 | 2 | 3 | 4 | 5 | 6 | 7 | 8 | 9 | 10 |

Skill: reviewing the numbers 1 to 10

57

Count and color 1 , 2 🐴, 3 🐕, and 4 🐑.

Count and color 5 , 6 🌳, and 7 🐟.

60

Count and color 8 , 9 , and 10 .

I Know My Numbers!

name

does a super job at counting!

Page 6

Page 7

I Know Numbers

Peel off stickers and place them where they belong.

Page 12

Page 13

Page 24

Page 25